OH AMERICA!

Memorial Poems to John F. Kennedy

Poetry and Illustrations

DORIS "JOY" THURSTON

NORVEGA PRESS

Oh America! Memorial Poems to John F. Kennedy

ISBN: 1886137021
ISBN 13: 9781886137028
Library of Congress Control Number: 2013920532
Norvega Press, Stuart, FL

Summary: Captures the world-felt crisis of John F. Kennedy's assassination in deeply spiritual prose-poetry accompanied by incisive scratchboard drawings.

Published by Norvega Press
842 SE St. Lucie Boulevard
Stuart, FL. 34996
Tdorisart@aol.com
Website: DorisThurstonArts.com

BOOKS BY AUTHOR/ARTIST, DORIS "JOY" THURSTON

Norvega Press

*(Indicates illustrated works)

POETRY

*The Temple Within: Sonnets and Asanas

NON FICTION

*A WAC Looks Back: Recollections and Poems of WWII
*The Beatitudes: Meditations and Prayers (spiral bound)

BIOGRAPHPY

Notes on Oskar Kokoschka
*Stroke! Trials and Triumphs Caring for a Father with Aphasia

FORTHCOMING

*A Yoga Tour of India with Swami Vishnu DeVenanda
*To Children, with Love

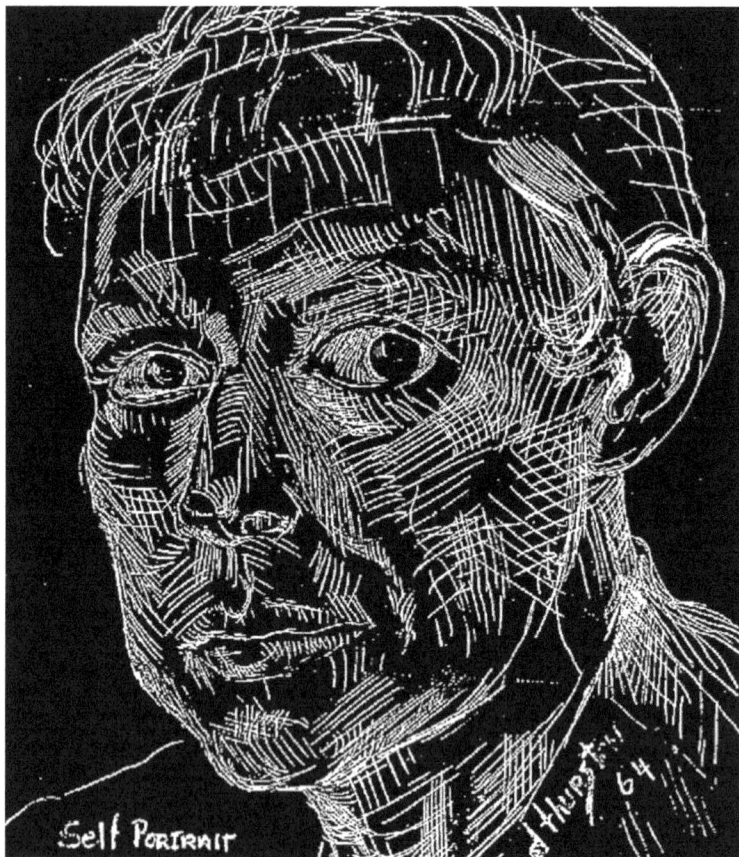

SELF PORTRAIT IN 1964

PREFACE

As an entertainer in show business for fifteen years, I combined song, dance, art, and comedy, performing from Greenland to South America. On November 22, 1963, I was preparing to sketch portraits for a convention at the Palmer House in Chicago. We received word that president John F. Kennedy had been shot. A stunned America was instantly overwhelmed with shock and grief.

Several days later I watched a program on NBC-TV entitled "In Memoriam." Famous actors read poetry against a musical soundtrack, as scenes of mountains, lakes, forests, seas, rocky shores and waves of wheat fields floated by. This was followed by the image of a little boy fishing — portraying the face of America.

Depressed, I wept profusely as words gushed forth too rapidly to write down. Turning on my tape recorder, I captured the following poems as they flowed forth, accompanied by the background music. Through these reflections, I had found a way to transform the president's senseless death into new "life," and the nation's healing process could begin anew.

I wrote in my diary: "This great tragedy to America has brought our country closer together in sorrow. Our monumental grief is symbolized by the tolling of the bell. Marching crowds solemnly follow the casket, which is draped with an American flag and drawn by six white horses. Boots hang backwards on a black, rider-less horse, commemorating our fallen hero."

Kennedy's killing was a modern-day crucifixion — and a monumental national tragedy. Never before in history had one man's death affected so many Americans. This one great man's passing marked the beginning of a very dark era of political assassinations in our country. The *effects* of these events would reverberate through the following turbulent decades. They would irreversibly alter the very essence of America's collective psyche and soul. Had it not been, what would our lives have become?

Today, fifty years later, mankind is still persecuting itself, while striving for the same values and ideals for which John F. Kennedy, his brother Robert, and so many others made the supreme sacrifice. The Cold War menace of nuclear annihilation has been replaced by the broader threat of Weapons of Mass Destruction, illicit drugs, guns . . . and, of course, the terrorists intent on using them. Yet we are still fighting and will continue to fight — for life, liberty, equality, and freedom to pursue happiness.

CONTENTS

ILLUSTRATIONS

OH AMERICA!

Memorial Poems to John F. Kennedy

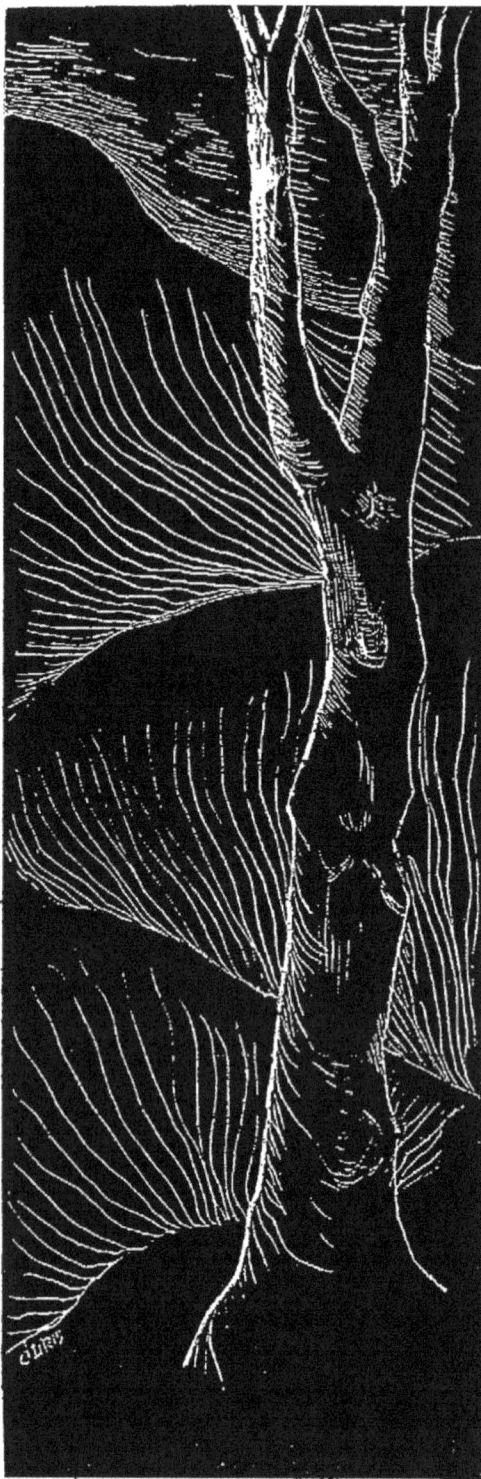

"The Silent Trees"

1. OH AMERICA

Oh America,
Thy woods, thy skies, thy wide gray plains
                    of rainy days

Thy spurts of laughter bursting forth
                    between the cacophony of sound
The silent trees and people onward moving
                    like the beat of the drums
                    when once the body wanes

Oh America,
                    so full of today
                    so full of sorrow
                    America

Today
You are one with the world
And this one day . . . the death of one man unites
                    the world
and we are reborn.

For we have borne together

and, renewed in grief
feeling freer, we are one, one more time —
Once again and yet, for the first time
                    we walk together
                    we smile together
                    we grieve together
                    we cry together

For in this death we have become
Somehow one.

Once more and yet again for the first time
the cloud bursts gone, the sun shines
behind the dark and white clouds . . .
. . . the rain is over, and once again . . .
We join the sun to laugh again . . . and hope

and pray,
each silently, today
with thee — the God that made us
all ONE

In the death of one man
who went back to return
                           to the God
                           which made him.

Oh America, I love thee too
I want to give the best of me
not only to thee, but to the world
that my words, my hands, my body
express the best in me
                    (for him to whom much has been given
                    must much give away)

Oh Lord, help me today
                    to find the better part of me
that I may give it back to Thee . . .

Oh Lord, thy winds, thy wide gray skies
The casket . . . into the ground . . .
                    is laid.

"And In This Hurt We Grew"

2. STRUCK DOWN

Struck down, struck down, Oh Lord
Struck down, he was
And in our hearts, we too were lowed
To our knees, we bowed
Deep within, the hurt
Became a part
Of all.

Struck down, Oh Lord
And in this hurt we grew
We grew stronger
And gradually we grew
Upwards towards thee
From our beginnings history made once more
A perfect line
And we saw what we are
And what we will become
And what we have become
We became.

Struck down, Oh Lord
And in one death we live again
Oh, thank you God for this majesty
For this new little thing that happened
And became so big . . .
Thank you, God, for giving us this one day
Of reality

For bringing us back to ourselves if only
For a brief moment.
Oh, help us to join hands
And become a part of ourselves that we may
Unite.

To begin
If only to begin
To begin again
To make the world free
To make the world a part of thy world

We can begin,
. . . "and the glow from that fire can truly light the world."
Let us begin . . .

"Oh God, Help Me"

3. LET THE LIGHT SHINE

Oh God, help me to see
Help me to see thy path,
Thy desire for me
Help me to move my fingers towards that
Which thou desirest for me.
Help me to be motionless
That I may be moved by thee.
Help me to feel nothing . . .
That I may become full
of thee . . .
That I may feel
That which thou would have me feel
For Thee, and for others . . .

Help my feet to traverse thy way
Help me to become every day a more perfect flower
With my roots deep in the ground
Always remembering
the sorrow
Always remembering the pain
Always remembering, Oh, God
that once again I, too, will be lowered

By thee, by man
To rise again.

Help me to bring the message to the world
The message that is THY message
That for every blackness there is light
That for every death there is a birth
That for every tree we see there is a root
That for every man, there is a mind
That can be comprehended
And a love that can be taken
And understood . . .

11

For every country,

> for every color
> for every nation
> for every woman
> for every man
> for every lighted window
> for every night . . . there is a day
> for every joy . . . there is a pain

Oh God, let me do thy will
And bring me to thee in LIGHT . . .
LET THE LIGHT SHINE
Let Thy light shine . . . through me
For Thine is the Kingdom
And the Power,
And the Glory
Forever . . . and ever . . . and ever . . .

> Amen

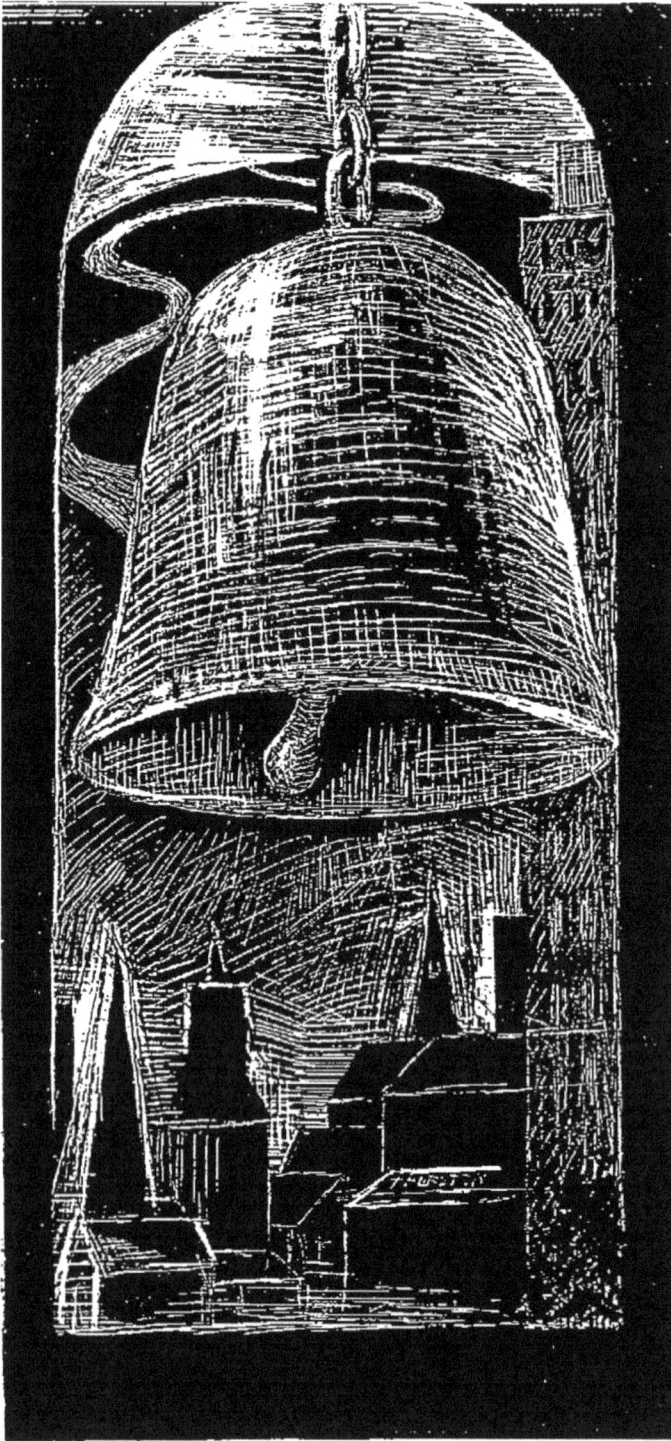

"The Tolling Bells"

4. OH LORD, THANK YOU

as the bird flies
as the night dies
as the ocean roars
as the dark becomes light
as the deepest pit has the highest cry
so has America arisen
to stand on her feet like a new-born babe
ready to walk again
ready to walk anew

the strong steel strength
of her tensile towers
the self-created application
of her cement power
her sinew-like, groping, grasping,
greedy limbs, stretching out
to touch, to reach
let us strive for the best that is in us
and find in ourselves
Thee.

the tranquility of
a little boy, fishing
the turbulence of autumn
descending after the summer
the stillness of the winter
as it comes to cover all,
the death-like splendor
that is in the coverlet of white

the vast majestic mountains
I have never seen
the colored rock
and the gray strength of Maine
the vast wheat fields of Kansas

the busy streets
seeking
                        to beat the clock . . .

The everydayness of what must be done . . .
the smoke-filled sky, the smoke-chilled room,
the olive green dirt as the blue shirt rests on his shovel
to view the passing train
the houses waken and become red, yellow, green,
                            blue
as the man collects tickets and waits for the snow

Oh bright, bright, bright, it all goes
into the night . . .
Oh wait, Oh listen, Oh see . . . what,
when you wait for it
Is not seen

And that is why the unexpectedness of this
tragic shock to a nation
has brought us back to the traumatic experience
of being born again,
has shaken us like an electric shock
has taken us up and sifted us down
has torn us asunder that we may be joined again,
each member to the other

Oh Lord, give me love
Give me the ability to communicate
to be that which I am
And the mountains stand
A monument
to what they are —
a part of us . . .

Let the mountains that are in me rise
and define themselves against the sky
                        of you

Oh Lord, thank you
for today
and yesterday
and the day before yesterday
and for the week that was
                    "Thank you, God."
Thou knowest thy plan
and the peak of the chapel with the tolling bells
all know
and become a part of the time
that is timeless
the time that becomes a part
of history
which becomes
Eternity

For Thine . . . is the Kingdom . . . and the Power
and the Glory of the world today.

"UPON A HILL"

5. A CRUCIFIXION

A crucifixion — upon a hill
A crucifixion — upon a street
A crucifixion — in time, out of time
A crucifixion, a falling to the earth
and a rising again of many people

One man falls but many rise
in doubt, in fear, in horror
but out of this horror
great Harmony
for the opposite of many colors
is the other color . . .
and in the end we meet in white
But these colors must be felt
as they must be united, and melded
together
each becoming a part of the other . . .
black meets white meets tan meets yellow
meets red (many races, many faces).

Oh Lord, when we have this perfection
will we be able to stand it? Or will we
then be meeting fire with fire
and be wiped out . . .
to join thee?

"IN OUR TOGETHERNESS"

6. THE LONG MARCH

Children in balconies
with mothers
                          sit
many faces
                          watching
                          waiting
All towards the great Amen . . .
                          (the folding of the flag).
the putting away of one personality

The flag is taken by a black guard
who hands it to an older man
who in turn presents it to Jacqueline Kennedy

The ranks and rows of men
in uniform . . .
standing alert, quiet
in front of rows and rows of cross-like graves
at Arlington

Many faces of America
Beautiful, young, wondering . . .
hats gently taken off in reverence
and the long, long march
towards the burial
when the spirit has long flown the body

It is us, the waiting
                          who worry
                          who wish
                          who wonder

who hope and who sorrow
It is him that is gone that gave us light . . .
the light that does not dim.

Only in the darkness can we see the light
we are struggling towards the light . . .
And the cardinal beats out his blessing
with stuttering voice
And we cross our chests, briefly
and with finality.

A montage of movement and stillness
A monumentality, a magnificence
A resurrection from the depth of sorrow
And in our togetherness, we die — to live again . . .
and Jacqueline places the light
        on the casket
        And all is one

        One world
        One man
        One hope
        One love
        and
        One Light.

"A Single Hope"

7. ONWARD AND UPWARD

Onward and upward
The thrust of my knowing
meets your thrust

Onward and upward
your knowing meets
my knowing

Onward and upward
at Capitol hill
today,
six white horses
And one lone black rider-less horse
                              (onward)
led the crowds

Led their laughter
their tears
their joys and their sorrows
and their fears were united
in one great tragedy
which has become
a single
hope
for America
and for the world.

Thank you, God.

"AS IF FROM THE CROSS"

8. MOTHERHOOD

arms that stretch
far into the world
reach out to every child
and flatten
against the plasticity of a
                    curved breast

The tree grows
upward and outward
so does the beneficial sun
of thy beauty
stretch into the infinity
                    of ever-present
                    newness

motherhood,
warmth of affection
protection . . .
deep asleep in beauty . . .
one cares, and knows
                    that mothers
                    are near

for what are mothers for
but to be mothers
what are women for
but to be lovers . . .
                    and mothers.

And left alone with God
and with her children
flanked on either side
Who knows what she cares for most . . .
                    this emptiness before her
or for the fullness — of the children at her side

27

He fell in her lap and she cried out,
                    "Oh, God, no!"
                    and he was taken.

As if from the cross
Christ fell
into the waiting arms
of the mother,
back to the beginning
the lover is the mother,
                    and together we are all
                    to all men . . .

to take and be taken
to love and be loved
to grow and having grown
to stay always
the child
and within the child
never to lose
never to tear away from
never to be alone

always to know
                    the mother

although the mother loses the child
the child never loses
the mother . . .

she stands alone without her child
the child, her lover
but the children will become
                    the Mother.

"WHEN LIGHT MEETS LIGHT"

9. LIGHT OF THE WORLD

(in the brief moment of his passing)

Light of the world
Let your light ever shine before men
That they may see your good works
And glorify your Father
which is in heaven
Let the light of your face
lift up your countenance
to other men
and grant them peace
Let the light of our faces
rise up together
and find peace
within
each separate entity
a related human being,
related to others . . .

And in the sunlight
of our birth
we see all men as brothers
and in the flickering light
that symbolizes each new death
We see forever in the gleaming light
the faces of those who have gone before us
the faces of those who are yet to come
the resolution that is the end
And the beginning . . .

the beginning . . . of
love
as seen through the light
of understanding

For all religions are one
All love is one
All life is one
In eternity life and death are the same
We go from birth to death
and from death to life
continually

And upon this hay,
this grassy earth . . .
under which lies a body, the body of
John Kennedy
Upon this berth of earth
imitation grass,
lies a light placed by other men
which symbolizes the love
in the souls of these men,
which symbolizes that light meets light
and when light meets light,
it puts out the dark

And now the door is closed
but life opens
for others
to know . . . their brother
                            (in this brief moment of his passing).

"IN THE BEGINNING"

10. LET US BEGIN

Oh the poetry that is in me
The poetry that is in thy world
The poetry that is in thy faces
The reality, the truth, that has
Been expressed in these three days
Is beautiful to see, and goes back
To the Liberty that we sought
In the beginning . . .
So let us now
BEGIN.

THE POETIC ARTISTRY OF DORIS "JOY" THURSTON

NOTE: All books below are spiral bound, soon to be available in digital format. (* = Illustrated)

1. NOTES ON OSKAR KOKOSCHKA (1955) *The author records Kokoschka's teachings and philosophy at Boston Museum School, Pittsfield, Mass. Cover illustration by Kokoschka. Booklet in Museum of Modern Art Research Library, NYC. (36 pages)*

2. *SONG IN THE WOODS (1955) *A woman finds respite in nature after an unrequited love affair. Poems and scratchboard drawings by the author reveal her transition from despair to enlightenment. (38 pages)*

3. *THE BEATITUDES: Meditations and Prayers ('64-'67) *"Your inspirational illustrations of the Beatitudes remind me of the sensitivity of Kaethe Kollwitz's work. Add the color paintings and you have a coffee table book."* (53 pages)
Andy McNiel,
Hospice Grief Counselor Stuart, FL

4. *POEM TO THOREAU (1974) *"You have captured Thoreau's spirit. An intuitive and spiritual walk around Walden Pond with handwriting and artistry intricately interwoven. I can use it in my classes."* 19 dwgs (56 pages)
Jim Reed, English Professor
Unity College, ME

5. *THE TEMPLE WITHIN: Sonnets and Asanas (1974) *"Couples highly crafted illustrations of Yoga asanas with heart-felt sonnets. This is my favorite!"* (44 pages)
Jim Reed, English Professor
Unity College, ME

6. *AUSABLE CHASM (1975) *"The gushing river rushing through a canyon in Keesport, New York, reminds me of the rivers of living water that flow through us and give us life."* Hand-written, with line drawings. (58 pages)
The Author

7. *TRAUMA TO TRIUMPH: Poems of a Caregiver (1989) *Describes her 12-year stint caregiving a stroke-aphasic father followed by her mother's fast disintegration. "I love your poetry and all of your books, especially 'Poem to Thoreau' and 'Trauma to Triumph.' I make a point to share them, as you tell it like it is with depth, compassion and insight!"* (74 pages)
Phyllis Kehoe
Port St. Lucie, FL

8. THIS PROUD EARTH: Poems of Maine (1989) *After her father's death, the author seeks solace in nature once again. Visiting the family cottage overlooking Penobscot Bay, she muses on the rhythms of life and death. (58 pages)*

Photos by Jean Englebach

9. *TO CHILDREN, WITH LOVE (1990) *A collection of children's stories and poems. Each could make a separate book of 32 pages. Ages 3-9 yrs. (102 pages)*

10. *MEMORIAL POEMS FOR WOMEN WHO SERVED (Oct. 1995) *After a 3-day dedication of the new Women's Memorial in Washington, DC, Doris was inspired to write a poetic summary of women who served in the military, from the Revolutionary War to Afghanistan. Lithographs accompanying the poems were created at Boston Museum School after her experience as a WAC during WWII. (50 pages)*

11. SONGS FROM A SEEDED SOUL: Collected Poems (2001) *From the 1950s to 2001. (92 pages)*

12. TURNING POINT: Poems After 50 (2008) *A culmination of unpublished and published poems. (79 pages)*

ABOUT THE AUTHOR

Award-winning portrait artist and poet, **DORIS "JOY" THURSTON,** of Stuart, Florida, is also a performer and painter of religious themes. Deeply moved by Kennedy's assassination, she wrote and illustrated these memorial poems. His death inspired her to choreograph a religious dance program entitled "12 Spirituals on the Life of Christ" for a Christian youth group. Twenty illustrations of these dances were exhibited in 1970 at the Interchurch Center of New York. Dancing the roles of Mary and Jesus led to a six-year search for the meaning of Christ's teachings in the Beatitudes from "Sermon on the Mount." Utilizing word, sound, color and movement, she created a series of twenty scratchboard drawings accompanied by prayers and meditations, which she later translated into large, dramatic oils.

The Archdiocese of New York invited her to choreograph a religious dance special for WOR-TV's "Point of View." Several Beatitude paintings are used as sets. The film is in the permanent collection of the Lincoln Center Dance Film Library. Her paintings have been exhibited in churches, libraries, museums and universities, including the Elliott Museum and Barry University in Florida, and the famed Christ Methodist Church on Lexington Avenue in New York.

After studying painting at Syracuse University (two years), she joined the Women's Army Corps (WAC's), during World War II (1944-1946), serving in three army hospitals as Occupational Therapy Assistant, Special Services Artist, and Entertainment Director. She sketched many portraits of wounded GI's, and toured as the lead in an original musical comedy about the WAC's. Continuing her education, she earned a diploma in painting from Boston Museum School, winning the Boit Drawing Award, and received a B.S. in Education from Tufts College (1949). Combining song, dance, and art in an original act, "Portraits in Song," she performed as "Doris Joy" from Greenland to South America.

Thurston's art and articles have been published in *Art News, the Chicago Tribune, Dance Magazine,* and *Saturday Review.* She has written *A WAC Looks Back: Recollections and Poems of WWII* (available at the Women's Memorial); *Stroke! A Daughter's Story*; an eBook, *The Temple Within: Sonnets and Asanas*; and *Notes on Oskar Kokoschka* (in the Museum of Modern Art Research Library).

Numerous national radio and television credits include interviews by such luminaries as Larry King, Studs Terkel, and Roger Mudd. She appeared on "CBS Evening News" with a painting of Rockefeller at the Republican Convention.

Her website is *DorisThurstonArts.com* and she may be reached at *tdorisart@aol.com,* or by calling (772) 283-5137.

www.ingramcontent.com/pod-product-compliance
Lightning Source LLC
Chambersburg PA
CBHW081231020426
42331CB00012B/3129